How to Care for Your Canary

CONTENTS

*We would like to thank the
following for permission to
photograph their stock:*
**Hansards Pet Centre, Romsey,
Roger & Anita Horwood,
Emsworth**

Photos by:
Naylor,
olin Jeal

KINGDOM

SELECTION

The canary hobbyist, whether a fully-fledged breeder and show participant or content simply with keeping a happy bird or two in a cage, requires a source of sound, accurate, and non-technical information covering the major aspects of the hobby.

This book was designed to fill this purpose, but it cannot substitute for the years of practical experience that an established breeder can offer. It is not always possible to acquire your bird from a breeder, but many specialist pet shops can offer an excellent selection.

The First Step

Usually, the first step in the initial purchase is to visit a pet shop and observe the various canaries. You should choose a clean, well-run pet shop with knowledgeable staff. Talk to the staff and get their opinion. Ask the seller for an assurance about the birds' singing ability. Not infrequently, the selected bird has arrived only recently and is not yet acclimatised to its new surroundings. However, once the bird is in your home, you can expect it to start singing within a week or two.

A male canary is more expensive to buy than a female.

Remember that it is the male canary who sings. Since, to the amateur, most young canaries look alike, particularly before the first moult, the ability to sing is frequently used to determine the sex of the bird. (The female also makes an excellent companion because of her pleasant voice and her ready adaptability to training.) Because females do not sing, they usually cost less. The price of a male is determined both by his type and the quality of his song. Remember that canaries, especially young ones, can be difficult to sex. If the staff at the pet shop cannot sex the bird and do not have paperwork from the breeder regarding its sex, they should be honest about their uncertainty. Be wary if all the birds you like happen to be male, or if the staff cannot tell you where the bird came from.

Canaries make very attractive pet birds.

The next factors to consider are the general health of the bird, the cage and cage furnishings, and the type of bird to choose.

Here is a brief checklist of signs of health you should be looking for in the prospective pet: **1.** A healthy canary is a lively canary. It is active in the cage and moves in an alert manner. **2.** Even if the canary is not singing, it will at least be calling and chirping. If the canary is healthy, its appearance will be clean and bright. **3.** A sick bird is quiet and listless. Its feathers are puffed up and it sits almost continuously on the perch. **4.** A canary with a cold shivers and sneezes. There is a slight watery discharge, and the droppings are white and watery. **5.** If the canary has sore eyes, it may rub its head against the sides of the perch or the cage bars. The eyes will be inflamed and reddish. **6.** Observe the general cleanliness of the pet shop where you intend to make your purchase and, in particular, the cleanliness of the prospective pet's cage.

What Type?

The next point is to decide on the type of canary. Since, at this early stage, the basic idea is to make your first purchase and start to get practical experience, it would probably be best to select one of the more readily available kinds.

Many of the more exotic breeds have died out simply because the general public was quite satisfied with the 'commercial' canaries sold in most pet shops. Many other varieties, bred in the past, have died out because of lack of popularity. Others are no longer bred because they were not hardy enough.

Border Canary

Most commercially-bred birds are Border canaries or Border mixes. The song of these birds is often far superior to the song of the more exotic types, which were originally bred for size and shape, or colour, rather than for voice.

The song of the Border canary is bright and cheerful, with crisp, bell-like tones blended with the notes common to the Roller canary. If a softer, Roller-type song is preferred, you will find that there is at least one bird with a softer tone in any group of singers. Take time to listen to the birds singing, returning several times if necessary, and eventually you will be able to pick out the softer-toned birds.

The size of the Border is 10-13cm. The colour of the plumage is bright yellow, yellow or yellow-and-green, but occasionally an all-green singer that is a throwback to the first wild birds may be found.

Red Factor

For many years, canary fanciers tried to develop a strain of red canaries. Many different wild birds with red plumage were mated with canaries but without success. Then in the 1920s the German breeder, Dr Hans Duncker, discovered that a small South American bird, the Red Hooded Siskin, would mate with the canary.

Since then, breeders have tried many combinations of these birds. However, it is only within the last decades that the strain has been perfected. These handsome newcomers can be found in all shades, from very light orange or copper to a deep orange-red that is almost pure red.

Other Varieties
There are many other varieties of canary from which you can choose; each has its own particular appeal. The following are some of the better-known varieties: Border Fancy, Norwich, Yorkshire, Gloster Fancy, Lizard, Frill, Roller, Fife and Crested.

A buff-coloured Border canary. Each variety has its own Standard of Excellence against which show specimens are compared.

CARE

At this early stage of your hobby, it is premature to go to such lengths as selecting an elaborate cage which blends in with the decor of your home. Many kinds of cage are available in many shapes and colours. These vary from about 30cm square to 60-90cm in length. The size and the degree of fashion is limited only by the amount of money you wish to invest. It is best to be guided by the advice of pet shop staff. The costs of bird, cage, cage furnishings and food are minimal. Here, too, the pet shop can save the hobbyist a considerable amount of time by giving proper and knowledgeable advice. You should be advised to purchase the following: a cage equipped with perches; three or four food bowls; grit and bird sand or paper; cuttlebone; birdseed; and treat food. Now let us consider each of these in some detail.

A pop-hole and landing platform can be used to connect a birdroom to the aviary.

Perches

The new pet needs several round or oval-shaped softwood perches in its cage. These should be of slightly different sizes so that the feet do not get tired from always gripping in the same position. You may even wish to provide the canary with a flat perch a couple of centimetres or more wide so that it can sometimes sit without having to cling at all.

Some natural perches will help to keep the bird's feet healthy. Do not make the mistake of adding so many perches that the bird has to fly through an obstacle course. Leave it a clear flyway so that it can get the necessary exercise. Also, check the perches periodically to make sure they are not loose and cannot turn when the canary alights.

Other Furnishings

The cage should have one bowl for food and another for water. One or two treat bowls, fitted to the wires of the cage, should also be provided. These are for treats and supplementary foods such as song food, conditioning food, and fresh greens. A cuttlebone should be hung close to a perch and changed regularly. This not only keeps the beak in condition, but also adds calcium to the diet. The floor of the cage should be covered with bird sand or paper.

Any new cage will be painted or finished with materials that cannot harm your bird. If you decide to repaint an old cage, or alter the colour of a new one, do not use a paint that has lead in it. Lead is as poisonous to birds as it is to humans. It is wise to avoid any oil paint. Use the latex types. Do not put your pet back into a freshly-painted cage too soon. Also, it is best to keep your canary in a room well away from the smell of fresh paint whenever your home is being redecorated.

Acclimatisation

Although canaries are highly domesticated, they are still capable of feeling ill at ease in new surroundings for the first few days. Your new pet has been subject to several changes in environment over a relatively short time and, therefore, requires a certain period in which to adjust. Until the canary shows signs of settling in, do not expect it to sing. For the first few days make sure the bird is fed and warm and allow it to get used to the household routine.

When you first bring the canary home, let it enter the cage by itself. Put the opened travelling-box against the open door of the cage and leave it there until the bird hops into the cage. If it will not go into the cage voluntarily, pick it up gently and put it into the cage. The bird must be picked up gently. Hold it from on top so that your hand covers the wings but leaves the feet free to move. Never grab a bird by the legs or tail or squeeze it to stop it struggling.

When your canary has become accustomed to its new surroundings, it will greet you and your friends with a cheery song. As with humans, canaries like sunshine and a light room. However, do not place the cage in direct sunlight. Make sure that no draughts reach the cage because chills are bad for birds and endanger their health. The cage should be covered from sunset to sunrise, particularly if strong artificial light is present. The bird's health and singing ability can be adversely affected if it does not get enough sleep.

A lizard canary - the greenish stripes are meant to resemble the pattern on a lizard's skin.

No matter what colour, posture or song your canary has, it will give you lots of pleasure.

Feeding

The canary fancier who decides to enlarge the scope of his hobby will soon realise the immense importance of proper diet. However, the foundations of proper nutrition are basically the same for both the pet and the more specialised breeding varieties.

In general, the canary requires a balanced diet consisting (like the human diet) of protein, carbohydrates, fats, vitamins and minerals. The only difference between the balanced diet you feed your family and the balanced diet you feed your pet is the source of the various nutrients.

The canary's meals should consist mainly of a daily seed mixture, supplementary foods and treat foods, and plenty of fresh water.

Seed Mixture

A canary's chief food is seed. The daily seed mixture consists of seeds grown specifically for canaries and is known simply as canary seed. It is a long, narrow tan seed, pointed at each end. Mixed with the canary seed are rape seeds, a very nourishing seed that canaries like, and an assortment of other seeds in small amounts that give the bird different flavours and extra food values.

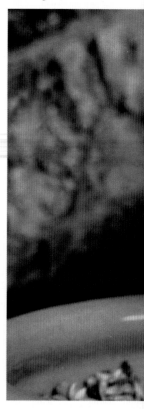

Give the canary fresh seed every day. It likes its food clean, fresh and sweet. Be sure that there is always seed in the bowl, and that it is seed! Canaries husk the seeds before eating them, frequently dropping the husks back into the seed bowl. This may give the bowl the appearance of being full when it contains nothing of nutritive value. Blow gently on the mixture and the light-weight husks will blow away, leaving the seed.

Supplementary Foods

Canary lovers have discovered that their pets appreciate and thrive on supplementary foods that help build resistance to sickness. Certain wild seeds are so appetising that finding them in their cages from time to time acts as a signal for the canaries to start a song concert. The popular brands of bird foods provide such supplementary treats in the form of conditioning foods, song foods, moulting foods, oat and groat mixtures.

Breeders have also discovered that eggs have value for canaries. A convenient way to provide the benefits of fresh egg is the commercially- prepared egg-biscuit food that can be fed in conjunction with other supplementary foods. All of the above can be given in the special treat bowls previously described.

Treats

Most canaries also relish certain treats such as biscuits or titbits that are actually a mixture of different seeds cooked with honey. Your bird will also enjoy sprouted seeds. You can easily grow these at home and serve them fresh. Remove the seeds after a few hours as sprouted seeds spoil quickly. Occasionally, a few well-washed greens can be given. The benefits of many varieties of fruit can be found in commercial mixtures that contain fruits in dehydrated form, mixed with seeds.

In case you have never fed a canary before, here is a word of warning about treats. The treat items that you give your pet should be specially formulated for canaries. Delicacies such as cake from your table are entirely unsuitable. If your pet becomes fat and listless, it will stop singing. The best singers are the birds fed on proper canary food with the supplementary foods that are real 'treats' for them.

**To achieve red plumage, a colour agent is put into the canary's seed when it is in moult.
Without this colour agent, the canary would be yellow.**

Cuttlebone

Minerals and salts complete the canary's diet. It can get these from a piece of cuttlebone, which is the internal calcareous shell or bone of the cuttlefish. A piece of this bone should hang in the cage at all times, soft side in. By picking at it, the bird keeps its bill sharp, and the calcium in the cuttlebone keeps its bones strong and its beak hard. You will have to replace the cuttlebone about once a month.

Water

Canaries love fresh water and they drink quite a bit so be sure that your pet is never left without it. During the summer months it is best to give fresh water twice a day.

Of course, your pet will want to drink from a clean bowl. Wash the bowl daily so that it remains as clean as your own china.

Grit

Bird grit plays an important part in feeding. Birds have no teeth; food is swallowed and stored in the crop. From there it enters the gizzard where the food is thoroughly ground up to optimise its nutritional values. For the gizzard to do its work efficiently, the canary must eat a little grit. Keep an ample supply in a bowl so that the bird can eat as much as it needs.

Housekeeping

It is vitally important to keep your canary's environment clean. Regular cleaning and disinfecting of the cage helps to keep your bird healthy.

Cage cleaning is very easy, requiring only a few moments of routine effort. Some of the basic techniques recommended by authorities on canary keeping are given below.

Every other day the bottom of the cage should be cleaned out and a fresh layer of bird sand supplied. This task is easier if bird sand paper is used to line the cage bottom. Paper also saves your pet from having to walk on the metal cage floor. Although bird sand contains grit, do not forget to provide a bowl of grit in the cage to ensure that your bird can obtain enough to aid its digestion.

Clean the perches every time you clean the cage bottom. Do not wash them, as the dampness can cause rheumatism, but scrape them with wire perch-scrapers available from pet shops.

Once a week, clean the cage thoroughly. Wash the walls and bars with a damp cloth or scrub them with soapy water. Then spray the cage with a mild disinfectant to keep away mites and other pests. Of course, during this kind of cleaning, you should put your pet in a spare cage. Make sure that the regular cage is thoroughly dry before returning the bird.

Baths

If your canary has a clean home, it will do much to keep itself clean. It will spend hours preening its feathers to keep them clean and well-arranged. As part of its plumage-care programme, see that your pet gets regular baths. In summer, allow it the health-giving fun of a clean bath three or four times a week, if not every day. In winter, about once a week is enough, but make sure the room is warm.

You can buy a little canary bath that attaches to the side of the cage, or you can put about a centimetre of lukewarm water in a shallow bowl on the bottom of the cage. Your pet will probably splash about and shake itself so much that it may leave a messy bath, just like a boisterous child. Then you will have to clean and dry the cage. Never keep a canary in a damp cage. If your bird is hesitant about bathing, splash a little water on it when you set out the bath.

Toys

Bird toys should be provided. These act as an outlet for your pet's natural instinct to pull things, and thus can help to prevent harmful feather-plucking caused by boredom.

A Canary cage with external bath and mirror/bell toy.

Health

Canaries are hardy birds that have lived so long in human society that man's dwelling has become their natural environment. If your canary is properly cared for, it will live a happy, contented life, filling your home with its cheery song. Your pet's resistance to disease always goes hand-in-hand with good care and proper feeding.

One of the best ways to avoid sickness in the canary is always to follow the rules for a well-balanced, nutritious diet.

Care is just as important as proper diet. This involves regular cleaning, including the cleaning of water and food cups, the bottom of the cage, perches and the cage itself. Canaries should be kept out of draughts, and should never be left out in the bright sun.

A heart-breaking accident may occur if your canary escapes from its cage, unless you take care to prevent it. Mirrors are dangerous because a bird may fly directly into them. Household appliances can endanger your pet. Unscreened windows and outside doors should always be kept closed if there is any chance of your pet escaping from its cage.

Ailments

Although canaries are generally hardy, they can be subject to some illnesses and diseases. If your pet behaves in an abnormal fashion, it can be an indication that it is not well.

If you suspect a problem, contact your veterinary surgeon for advice.

Natural perches are the most effective exercisers of toe muscles.

BREEDING

The most fascinating and creative aspect of canary-keeping is breeding. Breeding is the key to shows and to social meetings with other canary fanciers. Most important of all, however, is the sense of creative achievement derived from this activity. Whether the beginner starts with one pair in a breeding cage or several pairs in a breeding aviary is immaterial. In either case, both fun and possible profit are in the offing.

Experience—with success, as well as a few disappointments—is the only way to learn how to breed canaries successfully. Perhaps the biggest mistake any beginner can make is to become too enthusiastic and attentive towards his birds.

Remember, birds want privacy in which to carry out their parental duties. Do not show off the nest, the first egg and the nestlings to every visitor. Give your pets a proper diet and privacy and they will do all the work. Provide help only when they need it.

Dominant-white birds carry a lethal gene and so should never be mated to each other.

When To Start
The canary breeding season can start as early as February, but usually it is best to wait until the end of March or the beginning of April. This is especially true in particularly cold climates, even if your home is kept at an even temperature.

Probably the best canary for the beginning breeder is the Border. Borders are

Hen sitting on dried grass in a plastic nest pan.

hardy, all-round birds with beautiful plumage and a fine song. Let us assume that you have a fine male and want to buy him a mate. Your best move is to depend on a reputable dealer to select a good female of unrelated stock. Because genes are inherited from both parents, as much care should be used in selecting a female as in choosing a male. An excellent type male mated to a poor quality female is not likely to produce top-quality babies. It goes without saying that both parents should be of the same variety; for example, Norwich to Norwich, or Frill to Frill.

The science of genetics is much too complex to discuss here, but one point must be stressed: colourful plumage is only one desirable characteristic. You also want fine singing, good carriage and, above all, healthy birds. Selecting pairs on the basis of one trait only is not likely to pay off.

The Breeding Cage

The next step after selecting the birds is to provide a breeding cage, which can be purchased in pet shops. The best size is approximately 60cm x 60cm x 30cm. Ideally, the cage will have both a solid and a wire partition in the centre.

Provide the necessary seed and water cups and perches. Next comes the nest. Plastic nests are the easiest to clean and may be used over and over again. They can be bought from most pet shops.

Do not hang the nest too high or too close to the roof, or the parents will not be able to feed their youngsters. Remember, parent birds only feed their young when the young birds lift their heads and open their mouths, so they must be able to perch on the side of the nest with their heads just above the mouths of the babies.

No matter how tame your canary, resist the temptation to intefere too much in the rearing process. The parents usually know best!

Courtship

Now that you have bought your pair of canaries and prepared a breeding cage, you can look forward to having additions to the canary family.

What happens if you put the two birds in the cage and they appear to dislike each other or have a tendency to fight? This is where the commercial breeding cage comes in handy. Leave both partitions in the centre of the cage. Put the male in one section and the female in the other. After four or five days, take out the solid partition so that the birds can see each other. When they are ready to mate, you will hear their mating call, and the male will feed the female through the bars. Then you can remove the remaining partition. It is almost certain that mating will soon take place.

You will know when to give the female nesting material because she will start picking up feathers and any soft material she can find in the cage. At this time, provide short pieces of soft string or cotton, dried moss and grass, or even nesting hair. Caution: do not put long pieces of string or long horsehairs in the cage. Your bird may use them for the nest and, sooner or later, the parents or young will get tangled up in them, perhaps fatally.

Removing The Eggs

Replace each egg as it is laid with an artificial one, available from pet shops. Keep the eggs in a soft bed of cotton wool or soft cloth until the hen has laid her full number—from three to six. Then remove the artificial eggs and return the real ones to the nest, and let her begin to incubate them. This ensures that all the eggs will hatch at the same time. It is better for both mother and fledglings if the babies are all born on the same day, ensuring uniformity of size. Otherwise, the first baby to hatch would be much older and larger by the time the last egg had hatched. Incubation takes about two weeks.

Egg-Binding

Mother birds sometimes become egg-bound. The usual cause is insufficient exercise or the wrong diet. Get your birds in tip-top condition before breeding and you will not have this worry. The symptoms of egg-binding make the problem easy to diagnose. The hen will sit with her feathers puffed up in obvious discomfort. Later, her eyes will seem even more drawn and strained, and she will sit huddled on the floor. If you find a hen in this condition, you must act quickly.

A combination of heat and mineral oil is the prescribed treatment. Place a drop or two of mineral oil directly into the bird's beak and the same amount into the vent. Be careful not to insert the dropper too deeply or you may break the egg. Make sure the oil is down to the point of the dropper in order not to force air into the bird. The heat may be supplied in several ways. Probably the best way is to wrap a hot-water bottle in a towel and place the suffering hen on the towel. The heat should be over 38°C. This temperature is very warm to the hand, but the normal temperature of a canary is about 42°C. If you are in any doubt, consult a veterinary surgeon.

Should You Leave The Male In The Cage?

Canary breeders are not in complete agreement about whether to remove the male from the cage while the hen is incubating the eggs. If you want the male to sing, transfer him to a song cage nearby. Some males may not sing at all when they are with their mate in the breeding cage. If the male is young and without experience in nesting, he may annoy the hen. In that case, you should remove him from the cage and place him in a cage nearby. If you have only one pair, it is probably best to leave the male with the hen so he can help raise the youngsters, as long as he seems to be helping rather than annoying her.

Gloster fledglings, about 14 days old.

Feeding Young Birds

You do not have to do any of the work in feeding the young birds because the parents take care of it themselves. You should provide egg-biscuit food and nestling food so that the parent birds have suitable and nutritious food with which to feed their babies. Young birds are voracious eaters and require feeding at very frequent intervals throughout the day. Make sure that the special food you provide is fresh and accessible to the birds. This food is readily available at pet shops.

Occasionally, parent birds do not feed their young. This usually happens when both parents are young birds raising their first family. For this reason, it is wise to have at least one parent about two years old, preferably the female. This is a good point to remember when you are selecting a mate for your first canary and plan to breed them for the first time. Your pet shop probably can sell you a hen that has raised at least one family. If the parents do not feed the young birds, the parent birds should be removed from the cage. You will have to take over the task by hand-feeding.

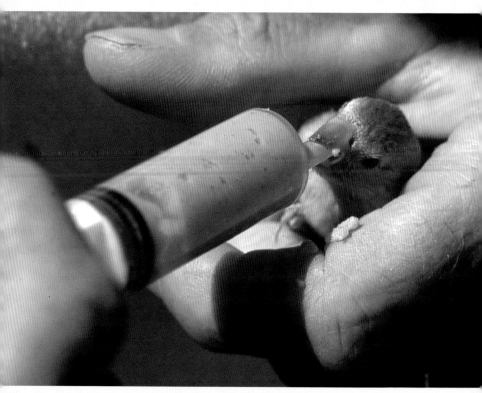

A youny canary being hand fed using a syringe

Moisten a combination of nestling food and egg-biscuit food and feed the baby birds from a small syringe or spatula. Probably you will not have any difficulty in getting the babies to eat because the slightest movement over their nest makes them open their mouths when they need food.

Hungry fledglings being fed by an adult on the nest

Like most songbirds, canaries can raise several families in the breeding season. One of the problems for the novice breeder is knowing when to remove the young from the first nest and when to stop the breeding. Young birds can be taken away from their parents when they are five or six weeks old. Continue to feed the egg-biscuit and nestling food but also start to provide regular canary seed mixture. Young birds often have trouble in handling hard seeds at first and may need some soft food for a time. For raising young canaries, many pet experts recommend egg food or egg-biscuit food along with the nestling food. Remember, however, that hard seeds

A broken-capped Gold lizard canary in excellent condition. Avoid over-breeding and and allow your birds to rest fully between clutches.

are the canary's natural food, and they should gradually be weaned to a seed diet. If they have trouble cracking the seeds, you can do it for them with a rolling pin — crack, don't crush.

The Last Nest

It is important to know when to allow the last nest. Some beginners are so enthusiastic about the fine youngsters their pets are raising that they let the parents breed as long as they want to nest. When the birds are paired early, they could have three nests by July. If the birds seem strong and healthy, the beginner is likely to permit one more nest. However, it is recommended that only one 'clutch' or set of eggs be permitted the first year. With more experience, you can decide whether the birds can stand the rigours of a second or third clutch the following year.

Moulting

Most birds, canaries among them, enter into moult immediately after breeding. Moulting is a perfectly normal condition and one that a healthy bird can go through with ease. It is not a good idea for the birds to moult while still raising their last brood. Give them a rest between the duties of a parent and the task of renewing their beautiful plumage for the coming year.

Warm climates trigger the moulting season, causing it to begin earlier and to finish earlier. Cool climates delay the moult, causing it to last longer. In most areas, the moult will be completed in about six weeks. Your usual regular care in keeping cages meticulously clean and ensuring the birds are away from draughts will usually see them through the moult without problem. A commercially-prepared moulting food should be provided at this time to ensure a proper diet. If the bird loses its feathers to such an extent that it has bald spots or loses its ability to fly, a vet should be consulted. This condition may be caused by a poor diet, parasites or an unsuitable environment.

Show Time

Many canary owners become so fascinated with their birds that they begin to breed them as a hobby. Once they have turned into serious breeders, it is only a short step before they want to raise specimens for show and exhibit the outstanding canaries from their breeding cages. Raising and training show canaries is a demanding but rewarding task.

For the novice breeder, the first step toward learning all about your new hobby is to attend canary shows and talk to other breeders. At the shows you can learn about the many varieties of canary and see them on the show bench. You will learn to tell the difference between a fine bird that is still only a beautiful pet and the show bird that wins prizes.

The best way to get started is to become an active member of a bird club. Experienced club members are always willing to share their knowledge with new

Your local canary club will help you decide if your bird is a good show specimen.

members. You can avoid many mistakes by accepting the advice that only an old hand can give.

Remember, a show specimen must be much more than a bird in perfect colour and good health. A bird is judged on many other factors, including size, depth of colour, contour and position. Particular attention is given to the bird's head, neck, shoulders and wings. In addition to having near-perfect birds, the exhibitor must train the birds so they do not flutter nervously or refuse to move correctly.

Your best canary may behave perfectly in the breeding rooms; it may accept the show cage readily. However, when you take it to its first formal show, the bird may flutter or fail to move properly. If this should happen, the judge will refuse to consider the entry despite its other merits.

To make show birds behave correctly you must train them carefully so that you know they will be at their best when shown. First, they must become accustomed to the show cage by being frequently run into it. A small training stick about 30cm long should be used to direct them from their regular cage into the show cage. Do not poke or touch the birds with the stick but use it often so that, when they see it, they know that you want them to move.

Show birds must become accustomed to strangers and be willing to let them handle the show cage. While you are training your pets, ask visitors to handle their cages quietly. In time, even nervous birds will learn to accept strangers.

As soon as you are convinced that you have birds of show quality, you should start their training. Since shows are usually held in the autumn, when canaries are in their finest plumage, you will want to have your birds well trained before the announced date. Once you are sure your birds are well trained, you can reduce the training time, but continue to use the show cage throughout the show season.

Grooming

All birds groom themselves and keep their feathers in top condition. Wild birds whose very life depends on the condition of their plumage spend hours every day preening their feathers. This means that you do not have to worry too much about the bird's appearance because it will attend to it very well itself. In the first months after moulting, a canary is at its best and requires little care. As the season wears on, however, the plumage may begin to show the effects of dirt and soot. Owners living in large industrial cities will be distressed to find their birds becoming increasingly dirty. In this situation, the only solution is to wash the birds.

Washing is a necessary evil, and it is exhausting for the canary. Frequent washing should be avoided, as it affects the colour and appearance of the plumage. However, it does have to be done occasionally.

The best way to learn how to wash a bird is to ask an experienced club member to demonstrate the procedure. The important points to remember are that the bird should be washed gently, rinsed thoroughly and dried carefully. The procedure should be carried out in a warm room absolutely free of draughts, with a drying cage kept very warm until the bird is thoroughly dry.

There is a special joy to be gained from breeding and showing your own stock.

IN GENERAL

Crooked and twisted feathers can usually be straightened by using hot water. Crests may sometimes lie raggedly after a wash and must be arranged into position.

In general, you will have to depend on careful breeding, good care, proper diet and the birds themselves, to produce acceptable show specimens.

Record Keeping

Keeping complete and accurate records is of vital importance to a breeder in any field. These records permit proper pairings and prevent matings that would weaken the stock. In a sense, these records are pedigrees since they allow the breeder to trace back the ancestry of each bird.

Records can be simple, but they should include at least the following information: the good and bad points of each bird; the date of mating; the number of eggs laid; the number of birds hatched; the number of birds raised.

Some of this information may appear unnecessary, but it is useful in improving the stock. Neglectful parents or bad feeders and birds that seldom produce a good number of young birds must be weeded out of the breeding stock.

Once a sound breeding stock is established, the records will help the breeder to continue producing fine birds. They will let you advise others how to pair birds purchased from you. When you want to buy additional birds, good records can assure you that your new birds are of unrelated stock and of the type you need.

In General

In earlier chapters we considered some of the basics of canary-keeping on a simplified 'how-to-do-it' approach. One thing must, by now, have become apparent to the reader: keeping a canary is a threshold to a much wider application of what has, for years, been one of the world's most fascinating hobbies.

There is not space in this publication to explore every aspect of canary keeping in depth, although we can discuss some of the more important areas in further detail. However, the best sources of information for the advanced canary fancier are other canary breeders, the various breeding and show societies, and the books written by the top authorities in the field.

Training

This activity, which draws on the talent, creativity and self-discipline of the breeder, requires a degree of patience not found very often. Training of the bird should begin at an early age: when it is about six weeks old. At that time, hang a show cage in the home aviary and introduce the young bird to it so that it becomes used to being on display and attracting public attention. The amount of time spent in the show cage must be built up slowly, starting with a few minutes, and not exceeding 30 minutes. Remember that the training stick should be used gently, as a guide to proper movement, not as an instrument of compulsion. Use it to induce the young

This show bird will have been trained from an early age to accept his show cage and inspection by a judge.

Your canary will benefit from attending small local events at the start of his show career before moving on to larger competitions.

birds to move into the show cage daily so they can be managed easily when the real competition starts. In about two weeks, the young birds should be conditioned to the show cage and emphasis on position training can then begin. Pet canaries can be taught to be finger tame.

If you are intending to train your bird in any way, remember the following guidelines: **1.** Start the training early, while the bird is still young. **2.** Finger train it first, then teach it more advanced tricks. **3.** A trained canary requires more food than an untrained one does. Use the treat-reward system to inspire it and keep it up to a high standard. **4.** Birds are extremely sensitive and go into shock easily. Therefore, never frighten the bird by losing your temper.

The crested canary appeals to many simply because it looks different than the common canary.

Once your birds have become accustomed to finger perching, you may be able to teach them some other basic tricks. Flying from a perch to your finger is easily achievable with patience, but do not expect your canary to cover great distances.

The following rules must be strictly adhered to: **1.** Never force a bird through an act; it if refuses, put it back in the cage and resume training the next day. **2.** Always reward the canary with a treat afterwards.

Finally, keep in mind that a tired bird cannot learn. Do not set too high a standard or continue the training sessions for too long.

Show Tips

One of the problems confronting the new canary hobbyist who seeks to enter the show world is the tendency to aim too high. It is wiser for the novice breeder to enter the less competitive local shows until he has gained experience.

One of the best reasons for concentrating on local events at first lies in the difficulty of travelling great distances to shows. Take into account such considerations as time, expense and the health of your bird before planning long trips. Be sure to visit a canary exhibition before attempting to compete in one. While luck is a vital, undeniable factor in any competition, the smart fancier leaves as little to chance as possible. Proper training of your choicest specimen, an impeccably presented show cage, and passable knowledge of competition etiquette and the breed standard help give your bird the best chance to make 'Specials', 'Best Hen' or 'Best Novice', or even a First!

Quite often, the show-oriented hobbyist is asked to help in the organisation of a show. The rôles here are many and varied, ranging from stewardship and public relations to secretarial work and actual judging.

Show personnel should be selected as many months in advance as possible. A good show is the result of good teamwork and the sooner the members of the team start working together, the better the show will be.

The Parisian Frill is one of the rarer canary varieties and is more delicate than the commonly known ones.

Lifespan

It is of interest to note that female canaries, owing to the loss of vitality during the breeding season, may not live more than five or six years. However, there are some canaries, apparently males, who have been known to reach the ripe old age of 16 years. One expert reports knowing of one that was 20 years old and still active.

Holiday Care

One of the most sensible things that a canary-fancier planning a holiday or business trip can do is to place his pet in the care of a pet shop that provides a boarding service. There the bird will receive experienced care and will not be subject to possible accidents or improper care by an inexperienced friend or neighbour. In most cases, the fee is nominal. Some pet shops even offer a 'visiting service' for the hobbyist whose stock requires attention while he is away.

Summer Care

Canaries should be kept in a room temperature of approximately 21°C and fed once daily. During excessively hot weather, give the bird fresh, cool water several times a day. Above all, keep the pet away from air conditioners and draughts. Both are harmful to canaries.

BIBLIOGRAPHY

THE PROPER CARE OF CANARIES
John Porter
ISBN 0-86622-447-5
TW-114
This book gives the reader all the basics of canary ownership, from selection to feeding, housing and health care. The specific needs of the various types of canary are also discussed.
Hardcover: 120mm x 174mm, 256 pages, full colour illustrations.

THE FIFE CANARY
Terry Kelly
ISBN: 185279-34-9
GB-091
The Fife is the smallest breed of canary, and although youngest it is now one of the most popular. The author has kept Fifes for over 20 years and in this book he provides detailed information about all aspects of selection, housing, feeding, health, breeding and showing.
Hardcover: 260mm x 180mm, full colour throughout.

THE GUIDE TO OWNING A CANARY
Linda A Lindner
ISBN 0-7938-2001-4
RE-201
This useful reference book contains information on selecting, housing, feeding, training and breeding these colourful birds. With sections on coloration and song canaries, this guide is certain to prove invaluable to novices and experienced owners alike.
Softcover: 170mm x 250mm, 64 pages, 75 full-colour illustrations.

CANARIES AS A NEW PET
Maja Muller Bierl
ISBN: 086622-529-3
TU-018
Written especially for those starting to keep canaries, this book includes all the essential information a novice will need to know in order to care for their pet.
Softcover: 175mm x 210 mm, 64 pages, full-colour illustrations throughout.

CANARIES:
SELECTING THE PERFECT BIRD
John Bernacki
ISBN: 07938-3080-X
RD-144
This book offers the reader a comprehensive reference for all the basic information a canary keeper will need, including selection, equipment, nutrition, housing and general health care.
Hardcover: 260mm x 170mm, 64 pages, full colour illustrations throughout.

USEFUL ADDRESSES

**Royal Society for the Prevention
of Cruelty to Animals
(RSPCA)**
Causeway
Horsham, West Sussex RH12 IHG
Tel: 01403 264181

National Council for Aviculture
4 Haven Crescent
Werrington, Stoke-on-Trent
Staffs ST9 0EY